AF553736

Also in Aleph 'Life Lessons'

'You Are the Supreme Light': Life Lessons from Adi Shankara

'Be Present in Every Moment': Life Lessons from Moinuddin Chishti

'The Light in All is One': Life Lessons from Guru Nanak

'Live and Let Others Live': Life Lessons from Mahavira

'Looking Within': Life Lessons from Lal Ded

LIFE LESSONS

'BELIEVE IN YOURSELF'

India has produced some of the world's greatest religious leaders, sages, saints, philosophers, and spiritual thinkers. They were monks, nuns, and renunciates, nationalists, and reformers. No one religion had a monopoly on them. They range from Mahavira and Buddha, who lived over 2,500 years ago, to medieval saints like Chishti, Avvaiyar, and Guru Nanak, to more recent philosophers and religious icons such as Vivekananda, Ramakrishna, Saint Teresa, and many others. The spiritual and philosophical heritage they left behind is India's gift to all Indians and the world.

In the 'Life Lessons' series we publish the essential teachings of some of India's best-known spiritual teachers, along with commentaries and biographical notes. Each book will be a handy companion to help the reader along the difficult pathways of life.

'BELIEVE IN YOURSELF'

~

LIFE LESSONS FROM

SWAMI VIVEKANANDA

EDITED BY

Nanditha Krishna

ALEPH BOOK COMPANY
An independent publishing firm
promoted by ***Rupa Publications India***

First published in India in 2020
by Aleph Book Company
161-B/4, Gulmohar House,
Yusuf Sarai Community Centre,
New Delhi 110049

ISBN: 978-93-89836-10-3

19 20 21 22 23 24 25

Printed in India

SERIES INTRODUCTION

India has produced some of the world's greatest religious leaders, sages, saints, philosophers, and spiritual thinkers. They were monks, nuns, and renunciates, nationalists, and reformers. No one religion had a monopoly on them. They range from Mahavira and Buddha, who lived over 2,500 years ago, to medieval saints like Chishti, Avvaiyar, and Guru Nanak, to more recent philosophers and religious icons such as Vivekananda, Ramakrishna, Saint Teresa, and many others. Each of them touched the lives of the people they lived among and the generations that followed. They inspired devotees and followers with their erudition and wisdom. The spiritual and philosophical heritage they left behind is India's gift to all Indians and the world.

Through the 'Life Lessons' series we will examine the teachings of some of India's best-known spiritual teachers. Each book will be a handy companion to help the reader along the difficult pathways of life.

Happiness and sorrow are unavoidable. The world is a place of trials and problems recur in every generation. Is suffering a necessary part of human life? How can one overcome suffering? Can hardship make a person stronger? What is happiness? Everybody wants to be happy, but how does one achieve this state? Does happiness come from vast riches and great achievements or does it come from the satisfaction of the soul? Is worldly success more important or is it fulfilment that one should seek?

These and similar questions vex every individual and have preoccupied the minds of philosophers and religious savants down the ages. The answers that these great souls found to life's conundrums occupy entire libraries worth of books and texts. This series is culled from their essential teachings and will present to readers some of the greatest truths to be found in India's spiritual heritage in a simple and accessible way. It is to be hoped that what you find here will prompt you to go deeper into the life and work of those who plumbed life's greatest mysteries.

Walking in the footsteps of these great men and women can take each of us to greater heights of knowledge, wisdom, and understanding. They can teach us how to find happiness and peace and the true meaning of well-being and success. Most of all, they can teach us how to value one another and cherish the holy gift of life.

INTRODUCTION

In September 1893, at the World's Parliament of Religions, Chicago, a young Hindu monk delivered a speech that cemented his position as one of India's most illustrious spiritual reformers and philosophers. Beginning with 'Sisters and Brothers of America', the historic address received a thundering applause from the audience and marked the rejuvenation of Hinduism.

The young monk was Swami Vivekananda,

born Narendranath Datta, the son of Vishwanath Datta, an attorney of the high court of Calcutta, and Bhubaneshwari Devi, a deeply religious housewife. His father's progressive rationalism and mother's religious devotion had a profound influence on young Narendra. His grandfather, Durgacharan Datta, a scholar of Sanskrit and Persian, had left home to become a monk at a young age. At the age of eight, Narendra was admitted to Ishwar Chandra Vidyasagar's Metropolitan Institution where he studied until his family moved to Raipur. In 1879, he enrolled at the Christian College, Calcutta, for a bachelor's degree, where he impressed his peers and teachers alike.

From an early age, Narendra showed a strong inclination towards spirituality and would often meditate before the images of Shiva, Rama, Sita, and Hanuman. He was torn between two irreconcilable desires: for social service and for renunciation. While he was initially influenced by Brahmo Samaji ideas of a formless God, rejection of idol worship, and a 'streamlined, rationalized, monotheistic theology strongly coloured by a selective and modernistic reading of the Upanishads and Vedanta',* he later came into contact with Western esotericism.

In his search for the divine truth, he would often ask people if they'd seen God. His quest to find an answer remained unfruitful until one day, in 1881, when after a long period of study, scepticism, and agnosticism, he posed the same

---

*Elizabeth De Michelis, *A History of Modern Yoga: Patanjali and Western Esotericism,* London: A&C Black, 2005, p. 46.

question to Sri Ramakrishna Paramahamsa, the revered saint of Dakshineshwar Temple in Calcutta. Sri Ramakrishna replied: 'Yes, I see him just as I see you here, only in an infinitely more intense way.'* This meeting proved to be a turning point in Narendra's life. Deeply intrigued by the Swami's personality, he began to visit him frequently at Dakshineshwar. He was initially sceptical about Sri Ramakrishna's teachings and often referred to the latter's visions as 'mere figments of imagination' and 'hallucinations'. Narendra constantly tested the saint, who countered all his arguments with patience, asking him to 'try to see the truth from all angles'.

---

*Swami Vivekananda, *Vedanta–Voice of Freedom,* Calcutta: Advaita Ashrama, 1991, p. 25.

Gifted with unique insight and intuition, Swami Ramakrishna Paramahamsa was able to gauge the potential of his disciple from the very beginning and, accordingly, trained him in the philosophy of Advaita Vedanta, whereby the individual Self was in absolute oneness with the Supreme. Narendra was deeply influenced by the life of Sri Ramakrishna and the philosophies of Vedanta. He was struck by Sri Ramakrishna's extraordinary spiritual powers, his absorption in God, his profound love and compassion, his childlike purity, his rejection of wealth and possessions, and his ability to expound the most abstruse philosophy in the simplest way. Narendra engrossed himself in the teachings of the Hindu scriptures until he understood their meanings. He realized that God could be with or without form. He accepted the message of his guru, of the universality of the Supreme Being, and of the importance of serving people in order to attain the divine Truth. Sri Ramakrishna taught him that the 'highest realization must hereafter remain under lock and key. You should not stay absorbed in personal joy. You will bring spiritual consciousness to men and assuage the misery of the humble and the poor.'*

Gradually Sri Ramakrishna helped him realize the power of samadhi (oneness with the Divine) and conquered him by spiritual force, and Narendra became the chosen disciple of the Swami. Narendra was ready to renounce everything to find God and he accepted Sri

---

**Swami Vivekananda Centenary Memorial Volume,* Calcutta: Swami Vivekananda Centenary, 1963, p. 455.

Ramakrishna as his guru. During the last year of Sri Ramakrishna's life, Narendra was constantly in attendance as a caretaker. As Sri Ramakrishna lay dying of cancer, he asked Narendra to take care of the other disciples and anointed him their leader.

In December 1886, Narendranath Datta became Swami Vivekananda. He along with his fellow disciples moved to a dilapidated house at Baranagore, near Calcutta, and started the first Math of the Ramakrishna Order. The new monastic order united a study of the sciences with religious meditation. The ideal of contemplation was wedded to the ideal of human service. Swami Vivekananda declared that the mandate of the Ramakrishna Mission was to serve the twin ideals of 'salvation for one's own self and for the good of the world'.

Two years later, he left the monastery and led the life of a wandering ascetic, travelling through the whole subcontinent as a parivraajakaacharya (wandering teacher), like another great Indian sage Adi Shankara* had done a thousand years earlier. He was filled with the desire to reconcile and assimilate modern scientific processes and speculation with ancient Hindu ideals. For five years, he travelled the length and breadth of the country; he lived with princes as well as paupers, unaffected by his companions or surroundings.

One evening, in the April of 1891, while

---

*See '*You are the Supreme Light*': *Life Lessons from Adi Shankara*, edited and translated by Nanditha Krishna, New Delhi: Aleph Book Company, 2018.

staying with the Maharaja of Khetri, his ardent admirer and disciple, Swami Vivekananda was invited by the maharaja for a nautch girl's performance. The Swami sent word that, being a sannyasi, he would not like to hear a nautch girl sing. Aggrieved, the girl sang a song of Surdas:

Thou art, O Lord, called the same-sighted.
One piece of iron is in the image in the temple,
and another, the knife in the hand of the butcher;
but when they touch the philosopher's stone,
both alike turn into gold.
*So, Lord, look not upon my evil qualities.**

The song wafted through the stillness of the

*Swami Tapasyananda, *Swami Vivekananda: His Life and Legacy,* Madras: Sri Ramakrishna Math, pp. 57–58.

evening and reached the ears of the Swami, opening his eyes to the great truth he preached but had himself forgotten. He realized there was no difference between people—rich or poor, nobleman or sweeper. This incident is reminiscent of the other great Advaitin Adi Shankara, whose encounter with a Chandala taught him a lesson about the equal vision of the all-pervading Brahman.

In 1891, he first heard of the forthcoming World's Parliament of Religions at Chicago. On 24 December 1892, he swam out to a rock* in the ocean off the coast of Kanyakumari, not

*The rock now houses a memorial known as Swami Vivekananda's Rock Memorial. It celebrates the spot where the saint received his vision for the future of India from the Mother Goddess.

even able to afford the boat fare. After three days of intense meditation, he obtained a clear vision of his mission: the renaissance of India, its upliftment from misery and poverty, and the need to reveal India to the West and vice versa.

From Kanyakumari he travelled to Madras where he was besieged by the intellectuals of the city who were clamouring for him to attend the Parliament of Religions. After much deliberation, the Swami became convinced that he needed to go although he had no resources to fund the trip. He awaited a sign from Sri Ramakrishna that he should undertake such a mission. He received this through a dream in which he saw his master walking towards the ocean, beckoning him to follow. After receiving the blessings and permission of Sri Sarada Devi, the Holy Mother (the wife and spiritual consort of Ramakrishna), he prepared for his journey abroad. Madras furnished his first disciples, supporters, and philanthropists who made it possible for the Swami to sail to America* and spread the message of Indian thought and philosophy to the world.

He reached Chicago in July—he didn't have any letters of introduction or sufficient money to survive on his own, but he was a man of destiny and providentially overcame all obstacles.

September 1893 saw his spiritual conquest of the World's Parliament of Religions in Chicago.

---

*My own great-great-grandfather, Pattabhirama Iyer, contributed a substantial amount to both Swami Vivekananda's trip to Chicago and to the construction of the Ramakrishna Mission in Chennai.

He carried the whole conference with him when he addressed that vast gathering as 'Sisters and Brothers of America', and proudly affirmed the timeless teachings of the Upanishads. This unknown monk from India made history that day.

After the conference, the Swami spent the next three years travelling extensively across America and England to deliver lectures, which were eagerly accepted by the people. During this time, he also established Vedanta centres in the US and UK. Swami Saradananda was given charge of the Ramakrishna Mission's work in America, and Swami Abhedananda, of the work in London. England contributed valuable friends and disciples—Captain and Mrs Sevier, Miss Margaret Noble, later known as Sister Nivedita, Sister Christine, and Sister Haridasi—who were all to play important parts in his work in India.

In 1895, he started an English language monthly magazine *Brahmavadin* (discourses on Brahman), which was published by the Ramakrishna Mission in Madras. The magazine covered spiritual and cultural issues until its eventual demise in 1914. He continued dictating his masterpieces on the four yogas, the teachings of the Upanishads, epics and Puranas, and composed hymns and poetry. He consecrated the Belur Math in 1898 and founded the Advaita Ashrama at Mayavati in Almora district in 1899. A second trip to the West in 1899 and unceasing work undermined his health.

Just like Adi Shankara, Swami Vivekananda's

achievements cannot be measured by the number of years he lived. He was dynamic by nature and disliked the idea of idleness. 'It is better to wear out than rust out,' he said. He wanted to die like a hero on the battlefield, working till the end of his life. Sri Ramakrishna had once told him: 'Now you know what you are. But the key to this shall be with me, and only when you have finished the Divine Mother's work, will you have it.'*

On 4 July 1902, at the Belur Math, the headquarters of the Ramakrishna Mission, the Swami meditated behind closed doors for three hours in the morning. Then he explained a verse from the *Shukla Yajur Veda* and took

---

**Prabuddha Bharata or Awakened India,* Swami Vivekananda Birth Centenary Number, Vol. 68, May 1963, p. 180.

a three-hour class on Panini's grammar for his disciples. Thereafter, the young man was ready to leave his body and continue his journey to moksha. He had tasted the bliss of nirvikalpa samadhi, the highest state of mergence with the Supreme Being and was now ready to merge with Brahman.

THE PHILOSOPHY OF SWAMI VIVEKANANDA

Swami Vivekananda's contribution to the revival and rejuvenation of Hinduism is immeasurable. He called Hinduism Vedanta, because he believed that Hinduism was the greatest among all religions, and Advaita Vedanta was the best that Indian religious thought could offer the world. Thus he gave it a new life. He wrote in

1896 that 'to put the Hindu ideas into English and then make out of dry philosophy and intricate mythology and queer, startling psychology a religion which shall be easy, simple, popular, and at the same time meet the requirements of the highest minds is a task only those can understand who have attempted it'* and he accomplished this to perfection.

Swami Vivekananda preached the philosophy of Neo-Vedanta—Advaita—which holds the Brahman as the ultimate reality. He defined the philosophies of Dvaita (dualism), Vishishtadvaita (qualified monism), and Advaita (monism) as different manifestations of the same truth, depending on the temperament and

---

**Letters of Swami Vivekananda,* Almora: Advaita Ashrama, 1942, p. 275.

ability of the student. He said that ignorance has to be eradicated for truth to reveal itself. The world is real. Vedanta does not denounce the world. It teaches the deification of the world and not its annihilation. He believed that ignorance and hatred were the root of religious fanaticism and, to counter them, made harmony a central pillar of his teachings.

Swami Vivekananda reconciled the different paths to liberation in his Neo-Vedanta. Instead of limiting himself to either jnana (knowledge), or bhakti (love), or karma (work), he combined them all in the ideal life and spiritual path. The main principle is given by him in his conception of Brahman: 'The Vedantist,' he says, 'gives no other attributes to God except these three—that He is Infinite existence, Infinite knowledge, and Infinite bliss, and he regards these three as One. Existence, without knowledge and love, cannot be; knowledge without love, and love without knowledge cannot be. What we want is the harmony of existence, knowledge, and bliss infinite."*

A crucial aspect of the Swami's Neo-Vedanta philosophy was acceptance of other forms of worship and the belief that all forms of worship, including the worship of God through rituals and physical forms, are acceptable. It is this principle that continues to inspire the Ramakrishna Math and Mission and their present-day humanitarian activities.

As an intellectual and a sage, he realized that

***Swami Vivekananda Centenary Memorial Volume,* pp. 275–76.

the philosophical approach of the ancient gurus, their quest for ultimate reality, the mysticism of the medieval period, the thirst for mukti (personal salvation), and the exuberance of emotional devotionalism were ending, and so he prescribed 'a new method of man-making', with humanity as its God and social service its goal or religion.

Swami Vivekananda said:

> Look upon every man and woman as God. You cannot help.... You can only serve. The poor and the miserable are for our salvation so that we may serve the Lord in the shape of the diseased, the lunatic, the leper and the sinner...

> The one thing that is at the root of all evils in India is the condition of the poor.... The only service to be done for our lower classes is to give them education, to develop their lost individuality.... Every nation—every man and every woman—must work out their own salvation...

The Swami was a staunch advocate of the enfranchisement of Indian women. Citing the well-known dictum, 'the gods are pleased where the women are happy', he promulgated the need for equal partnership between men and women. But he believed that this change must be distinct in its Indianness and not a mere imitation of Western standards. He believed education was essential and he was confident that with proper education, the condition of Indian women would also improve significantly.

Swami Vivekananda is also revered for being one of the makers of modern India. He awakened the nation into a state of self-consciousness. After centuries of neglect and oppression under the British Raj, the people were in a state of shock but he revived Hinduism in India and contributed to the nascent nationalistic thought.

Swami Vivekananda fostered Indian nationalism both in life and precept. His triumph in the World's Parliament of Religions at Chicago indirectly helped the cause of Indian nationalism by shaking up the Indian psyche and awakening the population to a sense of pride in their great culture. Hindus from Sri Lanka to Almora demonstrated, through their addresses, how their ancient religion bound them together by a sense of common heritage.

The Swami visualized a union between the East and the West through the exchange of Indian spirituality and Western knowledge. According to him, mere material development without a spiritual outlook would lead to terrible wars. Similarly, attaining only spiritual greatness would be meaningless for any country. Indians should try to be religious by realizing the great truths of their scriptures—by supplying food for the body and Vedic philosophy for the mind: 'Become an occidental in your spirit of equality, freedom, work, energy, and at the same time a Hindu to the very backbone in religion, culture and instincts.'

He abhorred weakness which he called

a sin and death. He condemned occultism and mysticism. He was against superstitions, preferring atheists to superstitious fools, 'for the atheist is alive, and you can make something of him'.*

The fundamental basis of nationalism, in the eyes of the Swami, was the cultivation of knowledge of the outside world on the part of Indians—a true grasp of the onward march of humanity. He didn't believe in a parochial view of patriotism and thus commanded universal respect and admiration. He did not consciously or unconsciously magnify his own religion and its spiritual ideas but also talked of the shortcomings in their practical application.

---

*Ibid., p. 500.

As a composer of songs and a very good singer, he won the blessings of Swami Ramakrishna and the plaudits of the learned. His simple and illustrative exposition of the Upanishadic doctrine of liberty, equality, and divinity enraptured his audience. Swami Vivekananda's historic speech at the World's Parliament of Religions in Chicago turned him into a celebrity in the West. The famous poetess Harriet Monroe records in her autobiography:

> But the handsome monk in the orange robe gave us in perfect English a masterpiece. His personality, dominant, magnetic; his voice, rich as a bronze-bell; the controlled fervour of his feelings; the beauty of his message to the Western World he was

> facing for the first time—these combined to give us a rare and perfect moment of supreme emotion. It was human eloquence at its highest pitch.*

The effect of his speech on the common men and women of America is melodramatically described in a poem entitled 'Aunt Hannah on the Parliament of Religions'.

> Then I heered th' han'some Hindu Monk,
> dress up in orange dress,
> Who sed that all humanity
> was part of God—no less,
> An' he said we was *not* sinners,
> so I comfort took, once more,

---

*Ibid., p. 541.

While the Parl'ment of Religion
roared with approving roar.*

The best statement of the power of Vivekananda's words was made by Romain Rolland: 'His words are great music phrases in the style of Beethoven, stirring rhythms like the march in Handel choruses. I cannot touch these sayings of his, scattered as they are through the pages of books at thirty years' distance, without receiving thrill through my body like an electric shock. And what shocks, transports must have been produced when in burning words they issued from the mouth of the hero!'**

Vivekananda was conscious of the growth

---

*Ibid., pp. 541–42.

**Ibid., p. 576.

of modern science and realized that modern civilization possesses many demonstrated truths and therefore more practical power. He said, 'experience is the only source of knowledge', and urged that the same methods of investigation that we apply to sciences and to exterior knowledge should be applied to religion. He said that Americans, instead of sending out Christian missionaries, should send experts of industrial education to India.

According to Swami Vivekananda, religion was not the cause of India's downfall; on the contrary, true religion was no longer to be found; customs, practices, and age-old rituals had to be replaced and a reshuffling and rebuilding of the forgotten spiritual heritage were urgently required to uplift the country.

The nationalism of Swami Vivekananda was based on intense patriotism. The luxuries of American life tormented him with thoughts of the miseries and sufferings of his countrymen; removing the wretched poverty of Indian masses haunted him day and night and even spiritual salvation was of less urgency than the alleviation of the condition of his fellow countrymen. This led to his doctrine—Daridra Narayana—which preached that service to the oppressed was the real service to God. He asked the youth to shed fear, gather strength, endure suffering, and sacrifice everything for the sake of the motherland and the service of her masses.

Several books by Swami Vivekananda have been published, and his complete works have been collected and published in eight volumes.

But the major portion of these eight volumes is made up of transcriptions of his lectures. He wrote a few articles and some portion of the book *Raja Yoga,* but apart from these, his English prose writings consist mostly of his letters of which, fortunately, we possess quite a large number. He was also a gifted poet: the force and vigour of his thoughts and imagery made his words effective. He did not write many poems, but a few were written during or after intense spiritual or emotional experiences, and these are among the best and most effective.

Swami Vivekananda was a harbinger of change, a breaker of bondage par excellence. He believed that the spirit was omnipotent and he wanted to see it applied in every sphere of life so that it would result in all-round development.

The soul had infinite potentialities that would automatically manifest themselves, he believed. His was a many-sided development: scholarship, knowledge, sharp analytical brain and depth of thought, vision, aesthetic sense, and a sense of humour. His eloquence and power of expression—both as a speaker and a writer—were powerful vehicles of communication.

Swami Vivekananda was also a spiritual leader who showed seeking souls the path to liberation and eternal bliss. He aroused a sleeping India and began the process of its rejuvenation. An accomplished orator, writer, and a poet, his achievements in these fields will also be long remembered. In his life and through his writings, Swami Vivekananda left a storehouse of materials to enlighten and uplift—a cornucopia of rich ideas and thoughts for everyday living.

Swami Vivekananda embodied in his life the motto 'If you want to find God, serve man.' His goal was to re-establish the ancient faith of the Hindus, to lead them out of the past and into the future, out of misery to a better life. Over a century later, his teachings remain just as relevant today as they were when he thundered his message to his countrymen and the world.

THE SEARCH FOR GOD

Vivekananda's guru, Ramakrishna, considered Brahman as the Divine Mother, the one who was everything, the Infinite existence, knowledge and bliss (sat-cit-ananda), the ultimate knowledge of reality. It is without a name, without a form and beyond space, time, and cause. The universe is the reflection of the Eternal Being, and is complementary to this indeterminate, impersonal being.

God is Infinite existence,
Infinite knowledge,
and Infinite bliss—
these three are one.
Existence without knowledge
and love cannot be;
knowledge without love, and
love without knowledge cannot be.
What we want is the harmony of existence,
knowledge and bliss infinite.

The poor, the illiterate,
the downtrodden—
let these be your God.

We are to see God in everything
and worship him.

It is not the God in temples,
symbols, and images
that we are to worship.
It is not the God in the high heaven,
whom we cannot see,
that we are to worship.

We are to worship the living God
whom we see before us
and who is in everything we see.
We are to worship God
in all men and women,
in the young and the old,
in the sinner and the saint,
in the brahmin and the pariah,
especially the poor, the sick,
the ignorant, the destitute,

and the downtrodden.
For the God in them
wants our worship,
our care, and service.

The practical side of Neo-Vedanta is
to see God in everything,
and as everything.
The earth, sky, fire, and water,
the sun, moon, and stars are
all forms of Brahman.
All men and women, and even animals
are forms of Brahman.
We are all children of the immortal,
ever pure and ever free.
Nothing can bind us,
nothing can defile us.

The Self is known to every one of us,
man, woman or child,
And even to animals.
Without knowing Him
we can neither live nor move,
nor have our being;
without knowing this Lord of all,
we cannot breathe or live a second.

The Vedantist gives
no other attributes to God except three:
He is Infinite existence, Infinite knowledge,
and Infinite bliss—
he regards these three as one.

Be pure and do good to others.
He who sees Shiva

in the poor, in the weak, and
in the diseased,
really worships Shiva;
if he sees Shiva only in the image,
his worship is but preliminary.

Unselfishness is the test of religion.
He who has this unselfishness
is more spiritual
and nearer to Shiva.

May I be born again and again
and suffer thousands of miseries,
so that I may worship
the only God that exists—
the only God I believe in,
the sum total of all souls,

my God of the wicked,
my God of the miserable,
my God of the poor
of all races, of all species.

Where would you go to seek God?
Are not all the poor, the miserable,
the weak God?
Why not worship them first?
Why dig a well on the shores of the Ganga?

I do not care for liberation or for devotion;
I would rather go
to a hundred thousand hells.
Doing good to others like the spring.
This is my religion.

Religion comes with intense self-sacrifice.
Desire nothing for yourself.
Do all for others.
This is to live and move and
have your being in God.

Each soul is potentially divine.
The goal is to
manifest this divinity within
by controlling nature—
—external and internal.
Do this either by work, or worship,
or mental discipline, or philosophy—
by one, or more, or all of those—
and be free.
This is the whole of religion.
Doctrines, or dogmas, or rituals,

or books, or temples, or forms are but
secondary details.

To understand Brahman we have to go
through the negation;
and then the positive side will begin.
We have to give up ignorance
and all that is false;
and then truth will reveal itself.
When we have grasped the truth, things
which we gave up at first
will take new shape and form,
will appear to us in a new light,
and become deified.

Thou art that (tat-tvam-asi),
we are all that.

Life is short
but the soul is eternal.
One thing being certain, death,
let us take up a great ideal, and
give up the whole life to it.
May He, the Lord,
who comes again and again
for the salvation of His people,
may He bless us and
lead us all to the fulfilment of our aims.

Worship the terrible!
Worship death!
All else is vain.
All struggle is vain.
That is the last lesson.
Yet this is not the coward's love of death,

not the love of the weak,
or the suicide.
It is the welcome of the strong man,
who has sounded everything to its depths,
and knows that there is no alternative.

I do not believe in a religion or God
which cannot wipe the widow's tears
or bring a piece of bread
to the orphan's mouth.

BELIEVE IN YOURSELF

To preach the doctrine of shraddha
or genuine faith is the mission of my life.
This faith is one of the most potent
of factors of humanity.
First have faith in yourselves.
Know that though one may be
a little bubble and another
may be a mountain-high wave,
yet behind both the bubble and the wave
there is the infinite ocean.

The old religions said
that he was an atheist
who did not believe in God.
The new religion says that he is an atheist
who does not believe in himself.

To succeed,
you must have tremendous perseverance,
tremendous will.
'I will drink the ocean...at my will
mountains will crumble.'
Have that sort of energy, that sort of will;
work hard, and
you will reach the goal.

Whatever we are now
is the result of our acts

and thoughts in the past;
and whatever we shall be in the future
will be the result
of what we think and do now.

Each work has to pass
through these stages—
ridicule, opposition,
and then acceptance.
Each man who thinks
ahead of his time
is sure to be misunderstood.

The road to good
is the roughest and steepest
in the universe.
It is a wonder

that so many succeed,
no wonder that so many fall.
Character has to be established
through a thousand stumbles.

The history of the world
is the history of a few men
who had faith in themselves.
That faith calls out the divinity within.
You can do anything.

FAITH AND STRENGTH

Vedanta recognizes no sin.
If there is sin, this is the only sin—
to say that you are weak,
or others are weak.

If there is a sin in the world,
it is weakness.
Avoid all weakness,
weakness is sin,
weakness is death.

That had been the great lesson
of the Upanishads.
Fear breeds evil
and weeping and wailing.
There has been enough of that,
enough of softness.

Anything that makes you weak physically,
intellectually, and spiritually,
reject as poison,
there is no life in it, it cannot be true.
Truth is strengthening.
Truth is purity.
Truth is all-knowledge.
Mysticisms,
in spite of some grains of truth in them,
are generally weakening.

Go back to your Upanishad,
the shining, the strengthening,
the bright philosophy,
and part from all the mysterious things,
all the weakening things.
The greatest truths
are the simplest things in the world,
simple as your own existence.

There is no misery
where there is no want.
Desire, want, is the father of all misery.
Desires are bound
by the laws of success
and failure.

If anybody comes to you
to speak ill of any of his brothers,
Refuse to listen to him in tote.
It is a great sin to listen even.
In that lies
the germ of future troubles.

Fill the brain with high thoughts,
highest ideals;
place them day and night before you,
and out of that
will come great work.

You are the children of God,
the sharers of immortal bliss,
holy and perfect beings.
It is a sin to call a man a sinner.

You are immortal souls, free spirits,
blessed and eternal.
You are not matter,
you are not bodies:
matter is your servant.

Have faith in yourselves
and stand upon that faith
and be strong.

Strength is life; weakness is death.
Strength is felicity, life eternal, immortal.
Weakness is constant strain and misery,
weakness is death.

Do not talk of the wickedness of the world
and all its sins.

Weep that you are bound
to see wickedness.
Weep that you are bound
to see sin everywhere,
and if you are bound to help the world,
do not condemn it.

What is sin,
what is misery,
and what are all these
but the results of weakness?
The world is made weaker every day
by such teachings.

Let positive, strong, helpful thoughts
enter into their brains
from childhood.

Lay yourselves open to these thoughts,
and not to weakening and
paralysing ones.

Never mind failures: they are quite natural,
they are the beauty of life.
What would life be without them?
Hold the ideal a thousand times;
and if you fail a thousand times,
make the attempt once more.

All the powers in the universe
are already ours.
There is no darkness around us.
Take the hands away and
there is the light.
Darkness never existed,

weakness never existed.
We who are fools cry that we are weak;
we who are fools cry that we are impure.

Make your nerves strong.
We have wept long enough.
No more weeping,
but stand on your feet
and be men.

You must not say that you are weak.
You know but little
of that which is within you.
For behind you
is the ocean of infinite power
and blessedness.

The only religion that ought to be taught
is the religion of fearlessness.
Either in this world or
in the world of religion.
It is true that fear is the sure cause
of degradation and sin.
It is fear that brings misery,
fear that brings death,
fear that brings evil.

Our young men must be strong.
Religion will come afterwards.
Be strong, my young friends;
that is my advice to you.

The will is stronger than anything else.
Everything must go down

before the will,
for that comes
from God himself;
a pure and a strong will
is omnipotent.

Truth is infinitely more weighty
than untruth;
so is goodness.
If you possess these,
they will make their way
by sheer gravity.

You must discard forever
self-aggrandizement,
faction-mongering, and jealousy.

You must be all-forbearing
like Mother Earth.
If you can achieve this,
the world will be at your feet.

LOVING AND GIVING

Who will give the world light?
Sacrifice in the past has been the law;
it will be for ages to come.
The earth's bravest and best
will have to sacrifice themselves
for the good of many,
for the welfare of all.

Ask nothing; want nothing in return.
Give what you have to give;

it will come back to you—but
do not think of that now.
It will come back
multiplied—a thousandfold—but
the attention must not be on that.
You have the power to give.
Give, and there it ends.

Our best work is done,
our greatest influence is exerted
when we are
without thought of self.

Self-sacrifice, not self-assertion,
is the law of the highest universe.

Be grateful that the poor man is there.
By making a gift to him
you are able to help yourself.
It is not the receiver that is blessed,
it is the giver.
Be thankful that you are allowed
to exercise your power of benevolence
and mercy in the world,
and thus become pure and perfect.

Man thinks that
he can make himself happy.
After years of struggle he finds out
that true happiness consists
in killing selfishness,
and no one can make him happy
except himself.

That which is selfish
is immoral,
that which is unselfish
is moral.

Learn that the whole of life is giving;
nature will force you to give.
So, give willingly...

Whether you will it or not,
you have to give.
The moment you say, 'I will not',
the blow comes; you are hurt.

It is love and love alone
that I preach,
I base my teaching

on the great Vedantic Truth
of the sameness
and omnipresence
of the soul of the universe.

It is nothing
until you have the heart to feel.
Feel for them
as your Veda teaches you,
till you find
they are parts of your own bodies,
till you realize that you and they,
the poor and the rich,
the saint and the sinner,
are all parts of one Infinite whole,
which you call Brahman.

This life is short,
the vanities of the world
are transient,
but they alone live
who live for others,
the rest are
more dead than alive.

Love never fails;
today or tomorrow
or ages after,
Truth will conquer!
Love shall win the victory.
Do you love your fellow men?

So long as millions live in hunger
and ignorance,

I hold every man a traitor
who, having been educated at their expense,
pays not the least heed to them.

Love is the only law of life.
He who loves lives,
he who is selfish is dying.
Therefore, love for love's sake
because it is the only law of life.
Just as you breathe to live.
This is the secret of selfless love,
selfless action, and the rest.

Happiness presents itself
before man,
wearing the crown of sorrow
on its head.

He who welcomes it
must also welcome sorrow.
What the world wants is character.
The world is in need of those
whose love is one burning love—selfless.
That love will make every word
tell like a thunderbolt.

Great things can be done
by great sacrifices only.

Liberation is only for him
who gives up everything for others.

There is no higher virtue
than charity.
The lowest man is he

whose hand draws in receiving;
and he is the highest man
whose hand goes out in giving.
The hand was made to give always.
Give the last bit of bread you have,
even if you are starving.
You will be free in a moment
if you starve yourself to death
by giving to another.
Immediately you will be perfect,
you will become God.

DIVINITY IS WITHIN US

Each soul is potentially divine.
The goal is to manifest this divine within,
by controlling nature, external
and internal.
Do this either by work,
or worship, or psychic control,
or philosophy, and be free.

The embodiment of freedom,
the master of nature,
is what we call God.

You cannot deny Him
because you cannot move or live
without the idea of freedom.

These prophets were not unique:
they were men as you or I.
They were great yogis.
They had gained this super-consciousness,
and you and I can get the same.
They were not peculiar people.
Every man must, eventually,
get to that state;
and that is religion.

No life will be a failure;
there is no such thing as failure
in the universe.

A hundred times man will hurt himself,
a thousand times he will tumble;
but in the end
he will realize that he is God.

In life and in death,
in happiness and in misery,
the Lord is equally present.
The whole world is full of the Lord.
Open your eyes and see Him.

Can religion really accomplish anything?
It can.
It brings to man eternal life.
It has made man what he is
and will make of this human animal a God.
This is what religion can do.

Take religion from human society
and what will remain?
Nothing but a forest of brutes.

Never did help come from anywhere
but from yourself.
In your ignorance,
every prayer that you made
and that was answered,
you thought was answered
by some being;
but you answered the prayer yourself
unknowingly.

The dwelling place of the jivatman,
this body,
is a veritable means of work,

and he who converts this
into an infernal den is guilty,
and he who neglects it
is also to blame.

Meditation is the one thing.
Meditate!
The greatest thing is meditation.
It is the nearest approach
to spiritual life.
It is the one moment
in our daily life
that we are not at all material.

Through the terrors of evil,
say my God, my love!
Through the pangs of death,

say my God, my love!
Through all the evils under the sun,
say my God, my love!

Thou art here, I see thee.
Thou art with me, I feel thee.
I am thine, take me.
I am not of the world's but thine;
leave not then me.

Worship everything as God.
Every form is His temple.
All else is delusion.
Always look within,
never without.
Such is the God that Vedanta preaches,
and such is His worship.

MOTHERLAND

In this land are still religion and spirituality,
the fountains which will have to overflow
and flood the world
to bring in new life and new vitality
to other nations, which are now
almost borne down,
half-killed, and degraded by political
ambitions and social scheming.

If you give up that spirituality,
the result will be that
in three generations
you will be an extinct race;
the backbone of the nation
will be broken,
the foundation upon which
the national edifice has been built
will be undermined,
and the result
will be annihilation all round.

The truths of the Upanishads
are before you.
Take them up, live up to them,
And the salvation of India
will be at hand.

The debt which the world
owes to our motherland
is immense.
Taking country with country,
there is not one race on this earth
to which the world owes so much
as to the patient Hindu,
the mild Hindu.

To many,
Indian thought, Indian manners,
Indian customs, Indian philosophy, and
Indian literature,
are repulsive at the first sight;
let them persevere, let them read,
let them become familiar
with the great principles

underlying these ideas,
and it is ninety-nine to one
that the charm will come over them,
and fascination will be the result.

I have said that we have yet something to
teach to the world.
This is the very reason,
the raison d'être,
that this nation has lived on,
in spite of hundreds of years of persecution,
in spite of nearly a thousand years
of foreign rule and foreign oppression.
This nation still lives.

The degeneration of India came
not because the laws and customs

of the ancients were bad,
but because they were not allowed
to be carried to their legitimate conclusions.

When you have men who are ready
to sacrifice their everything
for their country,
sincere to the backbone—
when such men arise,
India will become great
in every respect.
It is the men that make the country!

My life's allegiance
is to this—my motherland;
and if I had a thousand lives,
every moment of the whole series

would be consecrated to your service,
my countrymen,
my friends.

Three things are necessary
to make every man great,
every nation great:
conviction of the powers of goodness,
absence of jealousy and suspicion, and
helping all who are trying to be good
and do good.

Do not try to lead,
but serve.
The brutal mania for leading
has sunk many a great ship
in the waters of life.

What our country now wants
are muscles of iron and nerves of steel,
gigantic wills
which nothing can resist,
which can penetrate
into the mysteries
and secrets of the universe,
and will accomplish
their purpose in any fashion,
even if it means going down
to the bottom of the ocean and
meeting death face to face.

ARISE, INDIANS

Swami Vivekananda said: 'My whole ambition in life is to set in motion machinery which will bring noble ideas to the door of everybody, and then let men and women settle their own fate. Let them know what our forefathers as well as other nations have thought on the most momentous questions of life. We are to put the chemicals together; the crystallization will be done by nature according to her laws. Keep the motto before you: elevation of the masses without injuring their religion.'

Come, be men.
Come out of your narrow holes and
have a look abroad.
See how nations are on their march.

Do you love your country?
Then come,
let us struggle for higher
and better things.
Look not back, but forward march.
India wants the sacrifice
of at least a thousand of her young men.

You will revive the whole of India.
We will go to every country

under the sun.
Our ideas must be
a component of the forces
that are working
to make up every nation
in the world.
We must enter into the life
of every race inside India
and outside India.
We will work.
That is how it should be.
Say the Vedas, 'It is the strong, healthy,
of sharp intellect and young
that will reach the Lord.'

You must feel
for the millions of beings around you,

and yet you must be strong and inflexible,
and you must also possess obedience;
you must possess
these apparently conflicting virtues.

Liberty of thought and action
is the only condition of life,
of growth and well-being.
Where it does not exist,
the man, the races,
the nation must go.

Hero, take courage,
be proud that you are an Indian,
say in pride, 'I am an Indian,
every Indian is my brother.'
Say 'The ignorant Indian,

the poor Indian, the brahmin Indian,
the pariah Indian is my brother.'
Be clad in torn rags
and say in pride,
at the top of your voice,
'Indians are my brothers
Indians are my life.'

Do you respond
to the call of your nation?
Each one of you
has a glorious future
if you dare believe me.
Have tremendous faith in yourselves
which I had when I was a child.
Have that faith in yourself

that eternal power is lodged
in every one of our souls.

The great national sin
is the neglect of the masses,
and that is
one of the causes of our downfall.

No amount of politics
would be of any avail
until the masses in India
are once more
well educated, well fed,
and well cared for.

There is no chance
for the welfare of the world unless

the condition of women is improved.
It is not possible
for a bird to fly on only one wing.

This is the time to decide your future
with this energy of youth,
when you have not been worked out,
not become faded
but are still in the freshness
and vigour of youth.
Work—this is the time for the freshest,
the most untouched and fresh flowers,
alone to be laid
at the feet of the Lord.
Get up—greater works are to be done
than picking quarrels
and becoming lawyers, and other things.

Far greater is this sacrifice
of yourselves
for the benefit of your race,
for the welfare of humanity.

Who feels for the two hundred millions
of men and women sunken forever
in poverty and ignorance?
Where is the way out?
They cannot find light or education.
Who will bring the light to them?
Who will travel from door to door
bringing education to them?
Let these people
be your God...
Think of them,
work for them, pray for them.

The Lord will show you the way.
Him I call a mahatma (great soul)
whose heart bleeds for the poor,
otherwise he is a duratman (wicked soul).

EDUCATION

Education, education,
education alone!
Through education comes faith in one's self,
and through faith in one's self
the inherent Brahman is waking up.

Education is not the amount of information
that is put into your brain
and runs riot there, undigested,
all your life.

We must have life-building,
man-making, character-building
assimilation of ideas.
If you have assimilated five ideas
and made them your life and character,
you have more education
than any man
who has got by heart
a whole library.

Every nation—every man and
every woman,
must work out their salvation.
Give them ideas—
that is the only help
they require, and then
the rest must follow

as the effect.
Our duty is
to put ideas into their heads,
they will do the rest.

The great difficulty
in the way of educating the poor
is this.
...even if a free school is opened
in every village,
still it would do no good,
for the poverty of India is such
that the poor boys would rather go to help
their fathers in the fields,
or otherwise try to make a living,
than come to the school.

First bread and then religion.
We stuff them too much
with religion,
when the poor fellows
have been starving.
No dogmas will satisfy
the cravings of hunger...

If the poor boy cannot come to education,
education must go to him.
There are thousands
of simple-minded, self-sacrificing sannyasins
in our own country,
going from village to village,
teaching religion.
If some of them can be organized
as teachers of secular things also,

they will go
from place to place,
from door to door,
not only preaching
but teaching also.

We must have a hold
on the spiritual and secular education
of the nation.
A negative education or any training
that is based on negation,
is worse than death.

This mixture of life and death,
good and evil,
knowledge and ignorance
is called maya—

the universal phenomenon.
You may go on for eternity
seeking happiness.
You find much,
and much evil too.
To have good and no evil
is childish nonsense.

Life is a series of fights
and disillusionments.
The secret of life
is not enjoyment
but education through experience.
But, alas, we are called off
the moment we begin really
to learn.

This is the first lesson to learn:
be determined
not to curse anything outside,
not to lay the blame
upon anyone outside:
but be a man, stand up,
lay the blame on yourself.
You will find that is always true.

We want that education
by which character is formed,
strength of mind is increased,
the intellect is expanded,
and by which
one can stand on one's own feet.

Education is the manifestation
of the perfection already in man...
Knowledge is inherent in man.
No knowledge comes from outside;
it is all inside.

The end of all education,
all training, should be man-making.
The end and aim of all training
is to make the man grow.

Where parents are constantly
taxing their sons to read and write,
telling them that
they will never learn anything,
and calling them fools
and so forth,

the latter do actually turn out to be so
in many cases.
If you speak kind words
and encourage them,
they are bound to improve in time.
If you can give them positive ideas,
people will grow up to be men
and learn to stand on their own legs.

THE PATH OF ACTION

Karma yoga is the attainment of union with the Divine through work and action.

Karma yoga teaches us
how to work for work's sake,
unattached,
without caring who is helped,
and what for.
The Karma yogin works
because it is his nature,

because he feels that
it is good for him to do so,
and he has no object beyond that.

Each one of us is engaged
in some work,
but the majority fritter away
the greater portion of our energies,
because we do not know
the secret of work.

We must take into consideration
the great objection against work:
that it causes pain.
All misery and pain
come from attachment.
It is ninety to one that the human being

whom I have helped
will prove ungrateful and
go against me;
and the result to me is pain.
Such things deter mankind
from working.

Says the Gita: work constantly;
work, but be not attached; be not caught.
Reserve unto yourself
the power of detaching yourself
from everything, however beloved,
however much the soul might yearn for it.

Karma yoga teaches
where and how to work,
how to employ to the greatest advantage

the largest part of our energies
in the work that is before us.

Doing good to others
constitutes a way, a means
of revealing one's own Self, or Atman.
This is a discipline for God-realization.

We are all doing karma all the time.
I am talking to you: that is karma.
You are listening: that is karma.
We breathe: that is karma.
We walk: that is karma.
Everything we do,
physical or mental, is karma,
and it leaves its marks on us.

The secret of success is there:
pay as much attention
to the means as to the end.

The Gita teaches karma yoga.
We should work
through yoga (concentration).
In such concentration in action
there is no consciousness
of the lower ego present.

The result of every work
is mixed with good and evil.

Work for work's sake.

Be unattached.

Let things work.

Why should we do good to the world?
Apparently to help the world,
but really to help ourselves.

Work like a master and not as a slave.
Work incessantly,
but do not do slave's work.

Karma yoga teaches:
Do not give up the world.
Live in the world,
imbibe its influences
as much as you can.
But if it be for your own enjoyment's sake,
work not at all.

THE PATH OF DEVOTION

Love conquers all fear.
God is never to be feared
by those who love Him.
How can there be blasphemy
in the religion of love?
The more you take the name of the Lord,
the better, in whatever way
you may do it.

Bhakti yoga is
a real, genuine search
after the Lord.
A search beginning, continuing,
and ending in love.
One single moment
of the madness
of extreme love to God
brings us eternal freedom.

All is Brahman,
the One without a second.
Only the Brahman,
as unity or absolute,
is too much of an abstraction
to be loved and worshipped.
So the devotee chooses

the relative aspect of Brahman,
that is Ishvara—the Supreme Ruler.

Those who attain to that state
where there is neither creation,
nor created, nor creator,
where there is neither knower,
nor knowable, nor knowledge,
where there is neither I,
nor thou, not he,
where there is neither subject,
nor object, nor relation,
such persons have gone
beyond everything.

The teachers whose wisdom and truth
shine like the light of the sun

are the very greatest
the world has known.

The conditions necessary
for the taught are purity,
a real thirst after knowledge,
and perseverance.

Those who come to seek truth
with (such) a spirit of love and veneration,
to them the Lord (of truth)
reveals the most wonderful things
regarding truth, goodness, and beauty.

Bhakti yoga lays on us
the imperative command
not to hate or deny any one of the
various paths that lead to salvation.

If the devotional aspirant is sincere,
out of this little seed
will come a gigantic tree.
Like the Indian banyan,
sending out branch after branch
and root after root
to all sides,
till it covers
the entire field of religion.

Discrimination of food;
controlling the passions;
purity—through truthfulness, sincerity,
doing good to others
without gain to one's Self,
non-injury (ahimsa), strength,
a cheerful mind.

It is thus
that one may begin
to learn how to love the Lord.

When a man gets even higher
than that of mere thought,
when he gets to the plane of spirituality
and of divine inspiration,
he finds there a state of bliss,
compared with which
all the pleasures of the senses,
or even of the intellect
are nothing.

We see love everywhere in nature.
Whatever in society is good
and great, and sublime
is the working out of that love.

All things in the universe
are of divine origin and
deserve to be loved.

That man alone will be able
to get the best of nature,
who, having the power
of attaching himself to a thing
with all his energy,
has also the power
to detach himself
when he should do so.

THE PATH OF KNOWLEDGE

Jnana Yoga is the yoga of knowledge, of Brahman and Atman, and the realization of their unity. Where the devotee follows the promptings of the heart, the jnani uses the powers of the mind to discriminate between the real and the unreal, the permanent and the transitory.

First among the qualifications
for jnana, or wisdom
come shama and dama.

Shama consists
in not allowing the mind to externalize,
and dama,
in checking the external instruments.
Next comes uparati
or not thinking of things of the senses.
Then comes preparation—titiksha—
the most difficult of all.
The next qualification required
is shraddha—faith.
One must have tremendous faith
in religion and God.
Until one has it, one cannot aspire
to be a jnani.
Strong faith in God and the eagerness
to reach Him
constitute shraddha.

Then comes samadhana, or constant practise
to hold the mind in God.
The mind can be conquered
only by slow and steady practise.

Nityanityaviveka—discriminating between
that which is true and that which is untrue,
between the eternal and the transitory.
God alone is eternal;
everything else is transitory.
The universe is a mass of change.

He whom I have described to you
as the life of this universe,
as present in the atom
and in suns and moons—

He is the basis

of our own life,

the soul of our soul,

nay, thou art that.

Every soul is infinite.
Therefore there is no question
of life and death.

To the philosopher...

God is the life of his life,

the soul of his soul.

God is his own Self.

What at last remains

is God Himself.

If the soul be infinite,

there can be only one Soul,

and all ideas of various souls—
you having one and I having another—
are not real.

Those who dare to struggle
for victory, for truth, for religion,
are on the right path.
And that is what the Vedas preach.

What is this universe?
From what does it arise?
Into what does it go?
In freedom it rises,
in freedom it rests, and
into freedom it melts away.
All human life, all nature,
is struggling to attain freedom.

THE PATH OF DISCIPLINE

Raja yoga (considered to be the king of all yogas) is intended to achieve control over the mind. It is the ultimate goal of yoga practice, a state of peace and contentment that comes with sustained practice and meditation.

We have but one method
of acquiring knowledge.
From the lowest man
to the highest yogin,

all have to use the same method:
and that method
is called concentration.
The power of concentration
is the only key
to the treasure house of knowledge.

The power of attention,
when properly guided
and directly towards the internal world,
will analyse the mind
and illumine facts for us.

The powers of the mind
are like rays of light dissipated.
When they are concentrated, they illumine.
This is our only means of knowledge.

The goal of all raja yoga teaching
is how to concentrate the mind;
then, how to discover
the innermost recesses
of our own minds;
then, how to generalize their contents
and form our own conclusions from them.

There is no limit
to the power of the human mind.
The more concentrated it is,
the more power is brought
to bear on one point.

Believe nothing
unless you find it out
for yourself.

Truth requires no prop
to make it stand.

The yogi must always practise.
He should try to live alone.

Take up one idea.
Make that one idea
your life.
Think of it, dream of it,
live on that idea.

Others are mere talking machines.
If we really want to be blessed
and make others blessed,
we must go deeper.
We only get what we deserve.
It is a lie when we say

that the world is bad
and we are good.
It can never be so.

If you go on practising meditation for days
and months and years
until it has become a habit,
until it comes
in spite of yourself,
anger and hatred will be controlled
and checked.

Concentration is the essence
of all knowledge.
Nothing can be done without it.
Concentration is restraining the mind
into smaller and smaller limits.

First, meditation should be
of a negative nature.
Think away everything.
Analyse everything that comes in the mind
by the sheer action of the will.
Next, exert what we really are—
existence, knowledge and bliss—
being, knowing and loving.

The man who has practised control
over himself
cannot be acted upon
by anything outside.
There is no more slavery for him.
His mind has become free.

YOGA

Swami Vivekananda combined jnana, karma, bhakti, and raja yoga in his Neo-Vedanta. He envisioned 'a religion that will be equally acceptable to all minds; it must be equally philosophic, equally emotional, equally conducive to action'.

To become harmoniously balanced
is the ideal of religion.

And this religion
is attained by yoga—union.

The worker
is called a karma yogin.
He who seeks union through love
is called a bhakti yogin.
He who seeks it through mysticism
is called the raja yogin.
And he who seeks it through philosophy
is called the jnana yogin.
All these various yogas
should be carried out in practice.

Religion is realization,
not talk, not doctrine, not theories,
however beautiful they may be.

It is being and becoming,
not hearing or acknowledging;
it is the whole soul becoming changed
into what it believes.
That is religion.
Teaching should not contradict reason.
Such is the basis of all the yogas.

Equanimity of the mind is yoga.

Religion is attained by yoga—union.
To the worker,
it is union between men
and the whole of humanity;
to the mystic,
between his lower and higher Self;
to the lover,

union between himself and the god of love;

and to the philosopher,

it is the union of *all existence.*

The man who seeks after this kind of union

is called a yogi.